galatians
for freedom

A Bible Study

Connecting Hearts Publishing, Loveland, Colorado

Published by *Connecting Hearts Publishing*
©2016 Melissa Rhoads

ISBN-978-0692724668

CONTENTS

CONSIDER THE SOURCE

Read Galatians 1:1-5

I have always been a sucker for good-looking cars. Way, way, back when my husband and I were young and starting our careers, he thoughtfully let me decide which car to buy. My criteria were pretty simple. Budget, was first, but close second, okay, maybe even tied for first, was appearance. No large four-door sedan for me.

I went to the dealer and found a really good-looking used car in our budget. You may be wondering if consulting Consumer Reports played a part in my decision-making. No.

You can guess where this story goes, right? Yep. It goes where the tow truck will deliver. Right to the mechanic. As it turned out, my really good-looking car didn't look so good broken down on the side of the road. Had I checked Consumer Reports, I would have found red flag after red flag. I would have learned that this car ranked among the worst in terms of reliability. I should have considered the source. What looked really good and made sense in my decision-making process turned out to be not good at all.

We are about to embark on a study of a letter of the Bible written to the churches in Galatia. We know who wrote it. He identifies himself in the first verse and he gives his readers an opportunity to consider the source. Let's take a minute to look at the author and consider the source of the message. The good news, and it's no surprise, is that we are not going to come across any red flags here. This source both looks good and is good!

From reading Galatians 1:1, we learn that the author is Paul. Now read Galatians 1:1 and answer these questions:

1.   What does Paul say is his title?

2.   Who sent Paul?

3.   Who does Paul say did not send him?

So, now we know the source, right? In verse one, Paul calls himself an "apostle." According to Strong's Concordance, apostle means: "a delegate, messenger, one sent forth with orders." Paul was not speaking on his own behalf. Paul was representing, or speaking for, the one who sent him. Paul says, right in his opening greeting, he was sent by "Jesus Christ and God the Father." Paul made a point of clarifying that he was a delegate of God the Father and Christ the Son, not any human.

Just the first verse tells us a lot as we "consider the source." If we checked Consumer Reports, we would see that the source is 100% reliable because the source is perfect. Consumer Reports couldn't give even the very best of men that rating.

One of the first things Paul wants to convey to the church in Galatia, and to us about the one for whom he speaks is found in the first verse of Galatians. Read Galatians 1:1

4.   What does verse 1 say God the Father did?

That is power! God has power over life and death, he raised Jesus from the dead. He raised Jesus after Jesus had taken the punishment of death for the sins of every person in the world. Now we know the source for Paul's gospel message is ultimately powerful. More powerful than death, even death weighted with the burden of the sins of the world.

As we continue with the first few verses in Galatians, Paul tells us even more about the Father and Son source of the message. Read Galatians 1:3-5

5.   As a delegate, what are two things that Paul conveys from God the Father and Jesus the Son?
a.   _____and _____

6.   What two things do these verses say Jesus did for us?

7.   What was God's role in that?

Oh, the source is good isn't he? Just look at some of the verbs that describe his actions toward us: gave, rescued, and willed.

From a few verses, we have learned many things about the source of Paul's message. One last thing we see from these verses of Galatians is that all glory belongs to the source. Paul reminds us in verse 5 that the glory is to God forever. What does this mean? Strong's Concordance defines glory as: "opinion, judgment, view, splendor, and brightness."

Let's take a few minutes to reflect on the source of Paul's letter to the Galatians:

In the space provided, write down how you feel, knowing that the source of the gospel is:
- Giving. He gave his life to save us from our sins.
- Loving. It was God's will that Jesus save us.
- Powerful. It was by his power that Jesus was raised to life from death.
- Glorious. He is worthy of all good opinion and judgment. He is all good opinion and judgment. He is all brightness and splendor.

I find strength in knowing that the words in the Bible come from a perfect source, a source with unshakable integrity. Don't you? The Galatians must have felt so, as well. There was a reason that Paul chose to remind the Galatians to "consider the source" of his message, the gospel. We will get into that deeper in the study of the next verses.

God's word is so beautifully deep. There is so much to learn from just the first five verses of this book. Now let's take some time to apply a bit of what we've read here.

The Point:

Paul is not sent by men, but rather, by God and Jesus, whose intention and action is to save us from sin and the sinful world.

The Questions:

1. Why do you think it is important for Paul to point out that he is a delegate, or apostle, of God and Jesus?

2. What about work that you do? Do you serve ordained by God or men?

3. What do the following scriptures say about who gets the glory in godly service?

   a. Colossians 3:17

   b. 1 Corinthians 10:31

4. How does it affect you when you serve with God as the source, rather than pleasing others or yourself?

5. Verse 4 says that Jesus delivered us from the "present evil age." Who rules this present evil age? List ways you feel secure knowing that Jesus has delivered us from this age and its ruler.

6.   How does your life reflect that Jesus has delivered you from such?

7.   What (wickedness) do you want to be personally delivered from in this age? Based on what you know about your deliverer from Galatians 1:1-5, can you expect that he will deliver you and do so to perfection?

SCANDAL

Read Galatians 1:6-9

I still remember the cafeteria from my first year of high school. It was a big open "food court" surrounded by round tables that seated six to eight students each. I sat at the same table every day with the same group of people. Even without being labeled or assigned, certain tables were for certain people. It was an unwritten, but firmly held rule. From what my teenaged son reports, his middle-school cafeteria is not much different. He tells me that he is a "geek," which is apparently different from a nerd. In his vernacular, the geeks sit with the geeks, not the jocks and not the nerds. He would not think of crossing the line.

We draw lines, don't we? We have ideas, spoken and unspoken, about who can be part of our group, and who cannot. It is almost scandalous to cross those lines.

In September 1957, in the state I grew up in, lines were crossed, and appropriately so, in the name of equality and civil rights. To

cross those lines was so scandalous, the state governor ordered the National Guard to enforce the lines. Later that month, the President ordered the same guardsmen to make it safe to cross those lines. My grandfather was one of those guardsmen at Central High School, in Little Rock, Arkansas. The line was racial discrimination and the nine high school students brave enough to cross those invisible lines were known as the "Little Rock Nine."

It is such a strange thing to consider what the guardsmen present during that month experienced. One week they were preventing freedom and equality, then later they were commanded to protect freedom and integration.

Why do we draw lines? Maybe it is our effort to control our environment. Those lines protect us from what we fear. Maybe we fear that we are not good enough. Maybe, just the opposite, we believe we are very good, and that others coming near us would threaten our status. Maybe we draw the lines because we fear being dependent on something other than ourselves to define our goodness or worth.

There were lines drawn in the churches in Galatia. We read about them in Galatians 1:6-9. Lines were drawn in the name of religion, and according to God's word, the people drawing the lines were in the wrong. The line drawers were passionate. Passionate enough to send people to spy on the church in Galatia to find out whether they would submit to those lines. We will learn that the lines were putting a burden on the Gentile believers and perverting God's truth.

Let's read those verses and see if we can identify the specifics of this exclusionary group and their philosophy. We'll also try to figure out why Paul, commissioned to write the words of God, condemned the drawing of these lines.

Immediately after Paul finishes greeting the churches in Galatia, he begins to address the reason for writing the letter. Read verse

6 thoughtfully. One of the first things you see is that Paul says he is "astonished" at a choice that many of the Galatians have made.

1. What choice are many of the Galatians making in verse 6?

We find some pretty powerful words used in verse six to describe the Galatians' actions or choice and Paul's reaction to their choice. These words are: astonished and deserting, or turning renegade. Merriam-Webster online defines deserted (the Galatians' actions) as: "left unoccupied or unused." Synonyms include forsaken and rejected, and one near antonym is redeemed. In regards to his reaction, Paul uses the word "astonished." This word indicates the Galatians' choice surprised Paul.

I wouldn't be astonished, for example, to open the door to my teenaged son's room and find it messy. I would be astonished if it were clean. Why? Because it would be surprising, even shocking. Clean would be outside of what I consider his natural actions, and, therefore, astonishing.

Why such strong language? Take a look again at who and what they are deserting.

2. Whom does verse 6 say the Galatians are deserting?

3. What did Jesus call the Galatians to according to verse 6?

Therefore, we learn that the Galatians are leaving or forsaking Jesus, who called them to live in his grace. Grace, believe it or not, is also a strong word. It is strong by nature of what it is. It is a gift that can't be bought or earned. It is clemency. The guilty one receives the gift of not getting what he deserved! Let's take a moment to explore grace more deeply.

4. Read the following scriptures and underline what you learn about grace:

   a. Ephesians 2:8-9
       For by grace you have been saved through faith. And this is not your own doing; it is the gift of God, not a result of works, so that no one may boast.

   b. Romans 3:20-24
       For by works of the law no human being will be justified in His sight, since through the law comes knowledge of sin. But now the righteousness of God has been manifested apart from the law, although the Law and the Prophets bear witness to it— the righteousness of God through faith in Jesus Christ for all who believe. For there is no distinction: for all have sinned and fall short of the glory of God, and are justified by his grace as a gift, through the redemption that is in Christ Jesus,

   c. John 1:16
       And from his fullness we have all received, grace upon grace.

   d. Titus 2:11
       For the grace of God has appeared, bringing salvation for all people,

   e. 2 Timothy 2:1

> You then, my child, be strengthened by the grace
> that is in Christ Jesus

Just in these few verses regarding grace, we learn that salvation is through grace, and it is for all people. We learn that grace is a gift, and in being so, removes any boasting rights to our salvation. We learn that God's grace strengthens us. We also learn the depth of the grace. Scripture explains that grace is from the fullness of the Lord Jesus.

Take a moment to read Galatians 1:6-9 again. We already know that Paul is deeply upset about the fact that many of the believers in the Galatian churches aren't depending on Jesus' grace. We know it's disturbing because their choices reflect that that are deserting Jesus, forsaking grace and "turning to" what Paul calls a different gospel. Now let's take a deeper look at verses 7-9.

5.   What does Paul clarify about this different gospel at the beginning of verse 7?

6.   What words do we find in verse 7 that describe the actions of those trying to influence the Galatian believers?

7.   What phrase do you find repeated in these verses? Why do you think Paul, through the inspiration of the Holy Spirit, repeated this?

8.   What do these verses say is the ultimate state of those who are teaching a message that causes the Galatian believers to turn renegade to Jesus and his grace?

There is a great deal happening in the Galatian churches here. We read that there are people who have come into the churches and begun to teach, quite convincingly, that the Galatians must do something for salvation. Thus, denying the gift of grace that was, and could only be, given by Jesus. In the passages we read on grace, we learned that the true gospel teaches that salvation from sin comes only through the gift of grace. We learned that we cannot work to earn this salvation and we learned that grace was the gift of Jesus Christ available for all people.

In these passages, we find this group of religious people leading the Galatians away from the truth of the gift by trying to convince them that they must submit to certain aspects of the Jewish law to be saved from sin. Although Paul doesn't outright say that they are requiring submission to the law in these particular verses, we read about it specifically later in Galatians. He also gives us a clue that this is what is occurring in these verses with his mention of the angels. Look up Stephen's speech to the Sanhedrin in Acts 7. Pay particular attention to 7:53. We know that angels were often message bearers in scripture and as seen in Acts, were involved in the giving of the law.

9.   Putting together all that you have studied in Galatians 1:1-9, what seems to be happening here?

The Galatians are making life and death choices, aren't they? They had previously heard and believed the message of salvation and true freedom, the gospel. Now they are becoming confused and deceived by hearing another message. This alternate message

brings bondage and death. Those false messengers were known as Judaizers. They were trying to impose the Jewish laws on the Gentile believers. They were teaching that salvation required the Gentile Christians to submit to these laws. Why did this bring death? It was teaching that the Gentiles must "do" to be saved. Why is it so serious? Because the Judaizers were implying they knew what must be done to be included among the righteous, when the only way to truly be included among the righteous was and is to believe in and accept Jesus' sacrifice and his gift of grace. The Judaizers' teaching implied that an individual's actions could outweigh grace. They had failed to admit that there is no way that people can live a perfect life according to the law. They had failed to acknowledge their sinfulness before Jesus. They were relying on their own goodness and adherence to the rules when they could not maintain this standard.

You may wonder how Paul, a man passionate about sharing the gospel with everyone, a man willing to surrender his own salvation if that meant that his people could be saved (Romans 9:3) could say "let them be eternally condemned." I think he could have been pointing out the current state of a person who believes he is righteous by what he does. A person can never be righteous by her own actions. If a person depends on her own ability to keep the law, or salvation by her own good deeds, she will fail. These people are in a state of condemnation.

In reading these passages, we find two groups of religious people. One group is free and saved. They are the group living in the grace of Jesus. They are the group made righteous by their faith in what Jesus has done. They are an open group, accessible to all who believe in Jesus. The other group of religious people, although passionate, is bound and condemned. They are the line drawers. They are the group thinking they are in control of who is in and out. They are the self-righteous. They want to be the gatekeepers. Sadly, the only gate they open is to condemnation. In reality, they don't have the power to be gatekeepers. Only Jesus does! He has told us; He is the gate. The gate to eternal life. We enter through him alone. (John 10:7-10)

The whole idea that we are all equal seems scandalous doesn't it? None of us can be good enough to be perfect. We can't control who is considered good enough and who is not. It seems scandalous that every single person is not worthy of being in God's presence and yet every single person is worth Jesus' life.

The Point:

Jesus is the gate to salvation. We enter through his grace alone. We can never depend on our actions, or what we do, to save us. The great news, the true gospel, is that Jesus' actions are not only good enough, they are perfect. He has taken the punishment for our failures, and he offers us clemency.

The Questions:

1. Why would we want to believe that we can achieve perfection or be considered righteous by following rules?

2. Do we have trouble accepting the truth that we really are not good enough to be considered righteous?

3. Do we have trouble accepting gifts, especially, the undeserved gift of grace?

4. What do I teach/share about the gospel? Do I pervert it by telling others that there are things they must do?

5. What is grace? Why is Jesus the only one who can give it?

DIRECT EXPOSURE

Read Galatians 1:10-23

One of the reasons that our family moved to Colorado is to be close to the mountains. I love being able to see them. When we were house hunting, our favorite houses were those that offered even the tiniest glimpse of the mountains. Recently, due to the terrible fires burning in the northwest, a haze has descended over the mountains. In fact, although we live within a few miles of the foothills, some days I could not even see them. The mountains aren't the same through the haze. Sometimes they are not visible at all. The only way to really see the mountains clearly through the haze is to get right up in them!

We don't *need* a haze to entice us to enjoy beautiful Rocky Mountain National Park up close and in person. There are details and aspects of beauty that cannot be experienced from afar. I want to experience the mountains in their unobscured beauty.

In this next section of our study of Galatians, we will see how Paul experienced the gospel in this way. He was "right up in there." Paul tells us there was nothing obscuring his receipt of the gospel message but rather, he received it straight from the Lord Jesus. He was exposed directly to the source of all beauty, the divine, and it changed him.

Let's spend some time looking at Galatians 1:10-23 and see what we can learn about the revelation of the gospel to Paul and even God's revelation to us.

Read Galatians 1:10-23

1. Looking back at Galatians 1:6-7, who was teaching the Galatians in these verses?

2. Who did Paul say taught him the gospel?

3. What does Paul say about the method by which he received the gospel in verse 12?

Paul tells us in verse 12 that he received the gospel by revelation. Strong's Concordance tells us that the Greek word for revelation is apokalupsis, which means, laying bare, making naked, disclosure of truth, instruction concerning things before unknown; or used of events by which things or states or persons hitherto withdrawn from view are made visible to all, manifestation, appearance. Paul received the gospel directly from God and with full disclosure. It was not cloaked or hidden. It was bare.

4. Based on what we have learned about the people trying to distort the gospel to include a requirement for rule following, why is it significant that Paul received the gospel through a direct revelation from God?

5. What does this say about the authority of Paul's message?

Learning that Paul received the pure, uncloaked message from God reinforces that Paul's message was both pure and held ultimate authority doesn't it? The gospel Paul preached came directly from the author of the good news! It wasn't distorted or convoluted in any way.

After Paul establishes the purity and authority of the gospel message that he is preaching, he continues on to establish proof of how the grace message directly from Jesus completely saturated his being and effected change in his life.

6. List some proofs from verses 13-23 that show God's power and the credibility of the redeeming power of the gospel.

Paul made some huge changes! Or maybe we should say that Jesus made some huge changes in Paul! He went from a religious zealot and persecutor of believers in Jesus to the messenger of the gospel to the Gentiles.

7.   What do we learn about Paul's religious background before he met Jesus?

It is interesting to note that Paul had a very firm working knowledge of the Jewish law. He explains how he was way ahead of those his own age in his understanding and zeal in regards to the Jewish law.

At the writing of Galatians, we find him completely dependent on the grace of Jesus for salvation, not his own knowledge and not his religious zeal. Paul now likely had a better understanding of the law than those who were trying to force the law on the Galatians. I would submit that his understanding of the law was fuller because of the revelation of Jesus, who is the fulfillment of the law, and the indwelling of the Holy Spirit. Paul's fuller understanding added to his credibility and authority when he reminded the Galatians that they needed only to rely on Jesus for salvation.

Paul shares with his readers how the revelation of and the relationship with Jesus brought about change in his life. Before meeting Jesus, Paul was mature enough to have studied the law and he had begun to make a name for himself in zealously persecuting those who claimed that Jesus fulfilled the law. Interestingly enough, this turn around, or turn to Jesus, in Paul's life was in the works long before Paul knew anything of it. Read verse 15.

8.   When did God make plans for Paul's life?

Isn't that awesome! God knew and planned for Paul before Paul was ever born. God revealed himself directly to Paul and in that

moment Paul's life was completely given to Jesus, living in his grace.

Just like Paul was taught directly by God, I can be too. That is thrilling to me. I don't have to learn about God solely through others, I can be right with him. I do not have to look through the haze! I can be right up close and personal to his beauty.

The Point:

God's direct revelation of the gospel of Jesus to Paul completely saturated his being and changed his life. God desires to teach us directly and his revelation to us will effect change in our lives.

The Questions:

1.   Where did you, or from whom did learn the gospel?

2.   Read 1 Corinthians 2:6-16. List or underline some activities of the Spirit.

> 6 Yet among the mature we do impart wisdom, although it is not a wisdom of this age or of the rulers of this age, who are doomed to pass away. 7 But we impart a secret and hidden wisdom of God, which God decreed before the ages for our glory. 8 None of the rulers of this age understood this, for if they had, they would not have crucified the Lord of glory. 9 But, as it is written,
> "What no eye has seen, nor ear heard,
>   nor the heart of man imagined,
> what God has prepared for those who love him"—
> 10 these things God has revealed to us through the Spirit. For the Spirit searches everything, even the depths of God. 11 For who knows a person's thoughts except the spirit of that person, which is in him? So also no one comprehends the thoughts of God except the Spirit of God. 12 Now we have received not the spirit of the world, but the Spirit who is from God, that we might understand the things freely given us by God. 13 And we impart this in words not taught by human wisdom but taught by the Spirit, interpreting spiritual truths to those who are spiritual. 14 The natural person does not accept the things of the Spirit of God, for they are folly to him, and he is not able to understand them because they are spiritually discerned. 15 The spiritual person judges all things, but is himself to be judged by no one. 16 "For who has

understood the mind of the Lord so as to instruct him?" But we have the mind of Christ.

3.   Compare 1 Corinthians 2:7 to Galatians 1:15. When did God make plans for you?

4.   What do the following verses say about scripture or God's word?
      a.   Hebrews 4:12
            For the word of God is living and active, sharper than any two-edged sword, piercing to the division of soul and of spirit, of joints and of marrow, and discerning the thoughts and intentions of the heart.

      b.   Jeremiah 23:29
            Is not my word like fire, declares the Lord, and like a hammer that breaks the rock in pieces?

      c.   2 Timothy 3:16-17
            All Scripture is breathed out by God and profitable for teaching, for reproof, for correction, and for training in righteousness, 17 that the man of God may be complete, equipped for every good work.

d. Mathew 4:4
But he answered, "It is written, 'Man shall not live by bread alone, but by every word that comes from the mouth of God.'"

e. Ephesians 6:17
and take the helmet of salvation, and the sword of the Spirit, which is the word of God,

5. Based on the above scriptures (from questions 2-4), how can you understand the gospel and have the things of God revealed directly from God? (How can you be taught by God and not men?)

NOTHING TO ADD

Read Galatians 2:1-10

I shared a bit of wisdom with my 4-year-old just before we stepped out of the van to walk into this year's first day of preschool. It went something like this "Bennett, if you just look at mommy and smile, then I'll only have to take one picture and we can get it over with." He took it to heart! He stood there with his little body and giant backpack and looked and smiled! The picture taking this year was as painless as possible. Just 3 days earlier, my bigger boy begged me to take his first day of school picture the same way. His actual words were "take a picture like Papa, not like Nana." He asked for one and done!

The pictures are just part of it, though, aren't they? Of course, I sent them to Nana and Papa. In fact, that spawned a walk down first day of school photo memory lane. When looked at my teenager's first day of kindergarten picture, I had to chuckle. The funniest picture of the bunch was a picture of his back as he

walked into the school. It looked as if I had taken a picture of a backpack. You could barely see the top of a little boy head and two little legs poking out from behind the massive pack. That pack was huge and way too heavy. It's a wonder he didn't tip over backward from the burden.

Although that was cute, and slightly funny, the idea of being burdened to the point that we can't move forward is heartbreaking. Satan tries hard to do that. What power would Satan have if we realized that Jesus has completely set us free? Satan doesn't want to see us moving forward, or more specifically, heavenward, unencumbered. Satan hopes we will wear a pack that he can fill with so much weight that we tip over backward, arresting our progress and stealing our freedom.

We see this in the book of Galatians. There were people very intent on putting rocks in the Galatians' backpacks.

Remember is our previous study, we learned that Paul received the gospel of Jesus directly from Jesus in a revelation? Just as a reminder, the Greek word for revelation is apokalupsis; which means laying bare or making naked. This definition lends to some good visual imagery! The revelation Paul received was bare, naked. It had nothing added to it. No backpack full of laws. No actions that saved. This revelation of the gospel was the naked truth; Jesus saves, by his grace.

We are going to look at the first few verses of Galatians chapter 2. Paul gives further evidence for the naked truth and tells us what those false teachers were trying to put in the backpack.

Read Galatians 2:1-10

1.   What does Paul say caused him to go to Jerusalem in Galatians 2:2?

2. Whom did Paul go to meet with in Jerusalem?

3. What did he talk to them about? Why? (see Galatians 2:2)

We learn that after 14 years, likely marked from the date of his conversion to Christianity, Paul traveled to Jerusalem. He went with Barnabas and Titus to meet with Christian church leaders. He shared with them the message, specifically the gospel, he had been preaching to the Gentiles. He said he did this to ensure that his efforts and work were not wasted.

It is likely he was concerned about the Jewish Christians who were, as we learned from chapter one, determined to fill the Galatians' backpacks with the weight of Jewish law; working subversively to make the Gentile followers of Jesus believe that they had to be physically circumcised in order to be in right standing with God. This act of physical circumcision was to represent a believer's submission to the law of Moses.

Read the following verses:
2 Cor. 5:21
For our sake he made Him to be sin who knew no sin, so that in Him we might become the righteousness of God.

Acts 13:38-39
38 Let it be known to you therefore, brothers, that through this man forgiveness of sins is proclaimed to you, 39 and by Him everyone who believes is freed from everything from which you could not be freed by the law of Moses.

4. Based on the above, what causes people to be in right standing, or considered righteous, with God?

5. In whom are people truly set free from sin? What does not free people from sin?

It is clear from scripture that following the law won't set us free. We are set free by following the One who fulfilled the law. The church leaders had nothing to add to Paul's message because there was nothing to add. Jesus Christ *fulfilled* the law. This is the message of the gospel! It was given as a naked truth to Paul, nothing to add. Jesus is our righteousness!

6. Based on Galatians 2:3, what were the "false brothers" trying to impose on the Galatians?

7. What is the result of this imposition? Freedom or bondage?

We learn here that the false brothers were trying to get the Gentile Christians to be physically circumcised. It wasn't really the physical act that caused Paul to feel so strongly, however. It was what the action represented. If the Gentile believers chose to be circumcised, it would indicate that they were submitting to the law of Moses, or the Jewish law. We already know that Jesus

fulfilled this law and, in fact, set everyone free from the law by his grace.

Let's read just a little more about circumcision before we move on. If we do our research, we will learn that circumcision began with Abraham. This cutting away of flesh was a visual representation of the covenant between God and his people. Now read the scriptures below.

Deuteronomy 10:16
Circumcise therefore the foreskin of your heart, and be no longer stubborn.

Deuteronomy 30:6
And the Lord your God will circumcise your heart and the heart of your offspring, so that you will love the Lord your God with all your heart and with all your soul, that you may live.

Jeremiah 4:4
Circumcise yourselves to the Lord; remove the foreskin of your hearts, O men of Judah and inhabitants of Jerusalem; lest my wrath go forth like fire, and burn with none to quench it, because of the evil of your deeds."

Romans 2:29
But a Jew is one inwardly, and circumcision is a matter of the heart, by the Spirit, not by the letter. His praise is not from man but from God.

8.   What is the circumcision discussed in these verses?

9.   Who circumcises flesh?

10. Who circumcises the heart?

So, what can we learn here? Should these verses in Galatians be read only as a history lesson regarding the early church? One clear lesson is that the gospel of Jesus is the bare, unencumbered truth. Being right with God has been made free for all. This right status is independent or free of any work that we can do. It is independent of any rules we follow. That is freedom, indeed!

What about the issue of circumcision or following the Jewish law? I'm not really struggling with submitting to the law of Moses. But, I do find myself struggling with trying to submit to certain standards to define my worth and my righteousness, or my right standing with God. I am moved and encouraged to remember that only God can circumcise the heart and that only the bare, naked gospel of Jesus gives me freedom. It's time to ditch the backpack!

The Point:

Jesus is our righteousness. No one and nothing else can save. Only Jesus. When we submit to rules and even to other people in an effort to be right with God, we are truly in bondage.

The Questions:

1. Based on Ephesians 1:13-14 (below), what does Paul say is the evidence that we are now part of God's chosen people?

   In him you also, when you heard the word of truth, the gospel of your salvation, and believed in him, were sealed with the promised Holy Spirit, 14 who is the guarantee of our inheritance until we acquire possession of it, to the praise of his glory.

2. Who is responsible for circumcision of the heart?

3. Are there troubles in your life that you depend on something or someone else to fix? Explain.

4. How are you encouraged by remembering that only Jesus gives freedom? Freedom does not depend on nor can it by obtained by what you do. Who or whose rules you follow cannot earn your freedom.

SAFE IN THE LIGHT

Read Galatians 2:11-21

I have never liked conflict. I generally find ways to be passive or to sneak out of it altogether. Truthfully, because of my fear of conflict, I have always been stressed out by this next section of scripture. I usually just try to glance over it instead of having to think about and face the conflict in this passage. I feel my heart rate increase when I read about two transformed, redeemed people disagreeing.

God recorded this conflict for a reason. As I've studied it over the past few weeks, I've spent some time sitting with it and thinking about it. I admit I'm red faced and nervous still when I read this passage, but I also believe that God included this in his word for a reason. Thankfully, not everyone feels the same way about conflict as I do! Let's look at these verses together.

Read Galatians 2:11-16

1. What conflict do you find between Peter and the Gentile believers?

2. What conflict can you identify between Peter and Paul?

3. Was Peter's conflict with the Gentile believers a public or private event?

4. Did Paul's conflict with Peter occur in private or public?

That's some pretty intense conflict isn't it? (It is if you are "conflict phobic"!) We read that Peter, the apostle who had been known for his bold speaking in Acts 2 and his receipt of the direct revelation that the gospel is for all, had "withdrawn" from the Gentile believers. Peter did so when others, who were both Jewish believers and considered important, showed up. Paul calls Peter's behavior "hypocrisy." Paul feels so strongly that Peter's actions are wrong that he publicly and very directly confronts Peter about it.

There is not really much difficulty here in understanding why Paul called Peter out on this. Peter appears to be behaving out of fear of people rather than fearful respect for God.

Although conflict makes me uncomfortable, something in this story of Paul's confrontation of Peter gives me great comfort. I

haven't found any evidence in scripture that Paul and Peter continued in conflict on this matter. Nor do I find evidence that Peter continued to separate himself from the Gentile believers. I did not find any argument from Peter documented in this passage or elsewhere in the Bible. Unlike Peter here, when I'm personally confronted with a wrong, I generally argue. Maybe there is no documentation of Peter making an argument or continuing to disagree with Paul because this conflict caused Peter to realize his wrong. What I find comforting is that it seems to me that Peter, though called out and clearly in the wrong, found himself in a safe place. He was in a safe place, even a constructive place to look at his actions and motivations honestly. He was in a safe place to confess them and in a safe place to make difficult changes. What I mean by "safe place" is that he knew his standing with God. Opposite of those preaching and depending on their actions and perfectly following of the law in Galatians 1, Peter was saved by the grace of Jesus alone. Peter was not standing condemned. Peter was standing in the safe place of forgiveness. Because Peter's standing with God was that of forgiven and righteous, he could look at his actions without fear of condemnation. He could face his imperfections because his standing was righteous.

Let's also take a closer look at Galatians 2:17. Who Jesus is, is the very reason that Peter was in a safe place. Read verse 17.

5.   Based on what you read in this verse, does our sin affect Jesus' integrity?

That is a wonderful thought! Jesus is the I AM, the Alpha and Omega, the Way, Truth and Life. He is not changed nor is he compromised by our failures. He is not changed by our failures even when we claim him as our savior.

Jesus is. He offered himself, the fulfillment of the law, for our wrongs. When we are in him, just as Peter is, even when we are

wrong, He is our righteousness. Because of our state in him, we are safe to look at our wrongs and work on them. What a safe and saved place to be!

The Point:

It is in Jesus that we are made right with God. We are all sinners and all forgiven through his righteousness. We are equal in every way, in our sinfulness and our state in him. Our wrongs don't compromise who Jesus is.

The Questions:

1. Define justified.

2. Why do you think Peter might not have tried to "justify" his actions?

3. How does Galatians 2:16 say that we are justified?

4. Rewrite vs. 17 in your own words.

5. What does verse 17 say about the integrity of Jesus, even if we who have faith are found to be sinners?

6. Are there any specific things listed in Galatians 2:15-21 that we must do to be saved?

7. What are some of the things we try to do to be saved?

8.   Are they good enough?

9.   Read Philippians 1:6. Who can bring a work to perfect completion? Have I ever perfectly completed anything?

VERSUS

Read Galatians 3:1-5

A few weeks ago, my big boy was learning how to ride a motor scooter. He did great, most of the time. He poked along cautiously in our calm neighborhood. At one point though, he made a choice that was less than ideal. He slowly approached an intersection, and gently turned left onto our street. What he failed to do was look left. He pulled right out in front of a truck. Thankfully, the truck driver wasn't moving very fast and he just grinned a knowing grin at my son. He gave me a gentle look as well. I was quite thankful for that thoughtful driver! When my son made that decision to turn, I was just a few feet away. I witnessed his choice and I yelled out "Oh, Wesley!"

Have you ever been witness to someone making a terrible choice? A choice where there is only one right path? It's one way versus the other. Here in Galatians 3, we find such a choice and Paul is the witness. Not unlike me with Wesley, Paul uses an interjection

to address his beloved. In Galatians 3:1 we see this same interjection from Paul. Read the following verses in the ESV and look at how Paul addresses the Galatians here.

(Galatians 3:1-5 ESV)
O foolish Galatians! Who has bewitched you? It was before your eyes that Jesus Christ was publicly portrayed as crucified. Let me ask you only this: Did you receive the Spirit by works of the law or by hearing with faith? Are you so foolish? Having begun by the Spirit, are you now being perfected by the flesh? Did you suffer so many things in vain—if indeed it was in vain? Does He who supplies the Spirit to you and works miracles among you do so by works of the law, or by hearing with faith—

You can just hear the "parent" in his words, can't you? He starts the chapter by crying "Oh." After this interjection, Paul uses a word to describe the Galatians and their choices.

1.   What adjective do you see in Paul's first sentence?

2.   Define the word "foolish."

Merriam-Webster.com defines the word foolish as "lacking in sense, judgment, or discretion." It's clear from the next sentence why Paul would call them "foolish" and that is because they had been fooled. Paul uses the word "bewitched," which implies that the Galatians had been charmed or tricked. Paul then reminds them of the truth and that it is a truth not presented with smoke and mirrors. Look at verse one:

3.   What or who is the truth Paul pointed out to the Galatians?

4. How does Paul say this truth was presented to the Galatians?

Paul reminds the Galatians of the crucifixion of Jesus. This truth was clearly portrayed to them. I love this scripture because the truth, just by the nature of what it is, does not need a sales pitch. Truth can be presented clearly because of its own integrity. It can stand on its own. There is no need to give impressive arguments or flashy gimmicks to point out truth.

5. Read 1 Corinthians 2:1-4. What does this scripture say about how Paul presented the truth in Corinth?

6. What was Paul's message to the Corinthians? How is this similar to what was clearly portrayed to the Galatians?

Not only am I encouraged by this clear presentation of Jesus, the truth, I also love that Paul brings the Galatians right back to the only place they can be made righteous. That is to the cross of Jesus. He brings them here repeatedly. Reminding them that they cannot be made righteous by what they do. It must be a reminder of what they need. As I think about that, it must be a reminder of what I need. I need Jesus. I need to remember that he is the only way by which I can be made right, or righteous, with God.

Next Paul asks his spiritual children a series of rhetorical questions. These questions really highlight the choice that the Galatians have to make. They are the "versus" questions; this way versus that, right versus wrong.

7. List three rhetorical questions Paul asks the Galatians in the verses.

8. What are the opposing forces in the verses? (The versus in the verses?)

We read Paul asking his readers how they had been saved, how they received the Spirit, and how they had miracles worked among them.

Those trying to "bewitch" the Galatians would have them believe that all of the above happens because they follow the Jewish law and submit to circumcision under that law. They would have them believe that the supernatural and miraculous is happening because of their natural works. But Paul is reminding them, as in the previous chapters of the letter, that it is by faith in Jesus; the regenerate, life-giving death of Jesus and the indwelling of his Spirit versus the unregenerate works of the flesh, depending on submission to rules and practices for salvation.

In some ways I can relate to the struggle the Galatians were having. It is hard to live by faith that the Lord Jesus has done everything for us, submitting to crucifixion in order to fulfill the demands of the law regarding our sin. It's hard to grasp the idea that we are by nature sinful and that any failures to fulfill the demands of the law truly do separate us from God. Yet, the truth is so simple, not demanding elaborate arguments. The truth

simply demands faith. Faith that Jesus has done what we could not and cannot do. Faith that Jesus' death was the death of the perfect man and the death of God incarnate. Faith that this death was the fulfillment of the law and He has done this for once and for all.

The Point:

Righteousness, or being declared good by God, comes only through faith in Jesus. Sanctification, or being made more and more like Jesus cannot be worked into, but rather is a work of the Holy Spirit.

The Questions:

1. Look at Paul's words regarding Jesus in Galatians 3:1. He tells the Galatians that Jesus was clearly portrayed as crucified. Write down in simple language the facts you know about the crucifixion. Write down in simple language the reason for the crucifixion and what Jesus accomplished through this.

2. What are your basic beliefs about what makes you a "good person?"

3. What, or who, makes you a good person?

4. Read Galatians 3:5. Explain "the message" they heard using your own words.

PART OF THE FAMILY

Read Galatians 3:6-25

As far as I can discern, this next section of our study is chock full of deep stuff! I'm struggling to grasp it. So far, I've written two introductions with cute analogous stories, and they just aren't cutting it to sum up the concepts here. I've been really pondering, meditating and studying this section trying to understand what Paul is communicating to the brothers and sisters in Galatia and to us. As I now consider it, I realize that Paul actually provides an analogy to clarify some of his writing later in chapter 4. We will study it when we get to the end of that chapter.

So without further introduction, let's dig into this section of Galatians 3 together and see if we can come out on the other side with a little clarity. We just studied the first five verses of this chapter. In my mind, and actually in the previous chapter, I called them the "versus verses" because Paul asked the Galatians a series of questions. Paul asked them by which power Godly things had

occurred in their lives; by the Spirit or the flesh, by works or law? Now let's look at how Paul follows this. We'll pick up in Galatians 3:6.

Paul is about to speak about two different covenants, or promises, made to or with God's people. One was the covenant made with Abraham and the other was the law. Paul points out some significant differences in the covenants and hopefully, at the end of this section of study, we will understand some of those differences. What Paul shares with the Galatians is certainly significant to those in the community of faith, specifically faith in Jesus.

Read Galatians 3:6

1. Paul references one of the participants in the first covenant in verse 6. Whose name appears here and what does it say about him?

2. Who does scripture say is a child of Abraham based on Galatians 3:6-9?

3. What do these verses point out as the key element in being a child of Abraham?

There are some powerful and interesting statements here about faith! We see that Abraham's faith was credited to him as

righteousness. This does not say that Abraham lived a perfectly righteous life. If fact, we know he didn't. This said that God gave or credited Abraham righteousness because Abraham trusted in, adhered to, and relied on God's promises. Furthermore, we learn that even those who are not physical descendants of Abraham can be children of Abraham based on their faith. All people of faith in Jesus are benefactors of the blessing or promises made to Abraham.

4.   Re-read Galatians 3:8. What was announced to Abraham in advance?

5.   How are all nations blessed by the answer to number 4?

Father Abraham does have many sons (and daughters) doesn't he!

Let's keep moving through these verses and see if we can find out some information about the other covenant. In verse 10, Paul shifts from talking about the promise made to Abraham, the one that brings all of faith in Jesus into the family of Abraham, to the Jewish law. Take some time to read through Galatians 3:10-14. Look at some of the words Paul uses in reference to the Jewish law.

6.   List several points Paul makes in these verses about the Jewish law. I'll start with an example:
        a.   Gal 3:10 - All who rely on the law are under a curse.

b.   Gal 3:11

c.   Gal 3:12

Galatians 3:10 makes it very clear that if we think we can follow all the rules of the law perfectly, we are not only wrong, but cursed. Strong's concordance defines the word cursed as follows: "accursed, execrable, exposed to divine vengeance, lying under God's curse." We cannot achieve righteousness by following the rules, because it is not within our abilities. There is only one way that we will be credited with righteousness, and that is through faith in Jesus to redeem us from our sins (which equates to a modern-day version of violations of the law.)

Now let's take some time to explore these two covenants: God's covenant with Abraham, and the law.

God's covenant with Abraham is known as the Abrahamic Covenant. (Shocking name, I know.) We find it in Genesis 15. Take just a moment and read through Genesis chapter 15. For a little reminder of what happened before Genesis 15, I'll list a few points:
- God called Abram, whom he later named Abraham, in Genesis 12.
- God asked Abram to leave his country, people and father's house to go where God would show him.
- God made a promise to Abram that included several points. They were:
  - God will make Abram into a great nation
  - God will bless those who bless Abram
  - God will make Abraham's name great
  - God will make Abram a blessing

- • God will curse those who curse Abram
- • God will bless all peoples on earth through Abram
- • The promises did become progressively more specific and God promised Abram an heir.

In Genesis 15:6 we come across Paul's reference to Abraham from Galatians 3:6. In Genesis, we read "Abram believed the Lord, and he credited it to him as righteousness." What did he believe? He believed the promises that God had made to him! Paul will point out later in Galatians 3 that we are included in these promises, so we will come back to that. For now, though, the point that I want to explore is the nature of the promise that God made to Abram. This promise or covenant is known as an unconditional promise. Let's explore that just a little:

7.   Look up the definition of unconditional.

8.   What can be done to nullify this promise? (This is a trick question according to my teenaged son.)

9.   Who made this promise?

10.   Who were its participants?

Let's take a little time to explore the other promise or covenant referenced by Paul in Galatians 3. This is known as the Mosaic or

Siniatic Covenant. This promise is the one made to the Israelites after their delivery from slavery in Egypt. Details of this promise can be found in Exodus 19-24.

11. Read Exodus 19:1-6. Do you find an "if/then" statement in these verses? If so, write it down.

12. Based on verse 5, can you determine whether this promise is conditional or unconditional?

13. What is the promise? (see verse 5 again)

14. Who made this promise?

15. Who were its participants?

16. What could be done to nullify this promise?

17. If time allows, skim Exodus 19-24. This is the law to which Paul is referring to in Galatians chapter 3.

Whew, if you've boarded my train of thought and ridden this far down the tracks with me, you probably need a break! I'll try to wrap it up. Let's get back to Galatians 3 where Paul is talking to his friends about these two different covenants. You likely know by now, the Galatians were being led down a path, or bewitched, to be specific, to follow the Mosaic covenant. Remember from what you just studied that this covenant is conditional. The condition, which you recently wrote down as the "if/then" statement above, was that these commandments be kept.

Paul goes through quite an effort to remind the Galatians that they are actually under the other covenant. That is the unconditional covenant made with Abraham. In Galatians 3:15-20 Paul reminds them that one covenant is conditional and the other unconditional by pointing out that God alone was the one who put the Abrahamic covenant into effect.

When we think about the beauty of the unilateral, unconditional promise of God, it makes it worth all the studying and reading to get here! We, like the Galatians, are children of Abraham. We are under the unconditional covenant. Take a minute and re-read Galatians 3:6-9.

18.   How does verse 8 say that God announced the gospel in advance?

That is wonderful, isn't it! The covenant to Abraham foretold the gospel. That means that not only did God have the Galatians in mind when he spoke this promise to Abraham, he had us in mind! We, through Jesus, are a part of the unconditional covenant! I don't know about you, but it's a relief to me! I've read the law of

Moses and I'm sure I have not nor can I keep the law perfectly. In fact, I've read Jesus' explanation of the law in the Sermon on The Mount and I come to the same conclusion; I have not and cannot keep it perfectly. The good news, the "good tidings," the gospel, is that Jesus could, can and did keep the law perfectly. Not only did Jesus keep the law perfectly, he took my punishment for not keeping it. He fulfilled the conditions.

There is so much in to learn from these verses in Galatians. There is so much for which to be thankful! For now, I'm going to focus on the fact that I have been considered in advance, adopted into the family with whom the unconditional promise was made. This promise and family is destined for true life in God, because he has done the work. I'm already part of the family and therefore, I have no need to try to earn my way into this family. My way has been earned by Jesus, the fulfillment of the law. Even if I tried, I could not follow the rules to perfection, therefore nullifying the promise. I can't keep my "if/then." Thankfully, Jesus did!

The Point:

We are under the unconditional, unilateral covenant made to Abraham. We cannot be perfect enough to be righteous. Jesus is perfect enough to be righteous and in him, we are made part of God's family.

The Questions:

1. What actions do we try to make other people "do" to be called or considered "God's chosen" people? Who gets to choose who is God's chosen?

2. How do you feel remembering that God planned for you long ago and prophesied about you in Gen 12:3, 18:18, and 22:18?

3. Consider Galatians 3:8. It's for me and you. How do you feel about the glad tidings of a savior?

4. How was Abraham considered righteous? How are we considered righteous?

5. Read the Sermon on the Mount. Do you keep these parts of the law perfectly? Did Jesus?

6.   What is your standing before God based on your performance in keeping the law? Did the words "pretty good" flit through your mind? How true is that? Is there a sliding scale of holiness?

7.   What does Galatians 3:12 say about the person who is trying to be/do good enough?

8.   Based on verse 21, can following the Law give life? Who gives life? Write down some verses to support your answer.

9.   What does verse 3:23 say about the law? What was the status of those under the law? How would the idea of following the law translate to us today? If we are strictly adhering to and putting faith in our ability to follow the law, what is our status?

WEDDING CLOTHES

Read Galatians 3:26-29

The wedding dress. It's a big deal. We want it to be beautiful and magical; really just perfect. There are entire T.V. shows dedicated to finding just the right dress. There's a lot riding on the dress! It makes us feel and look beautiful, it is symbolic of who we are and what we present to our groom and it is an essential part of the wedding ceremony. The wedding dress is traditionally white, representing purity. My wedding dress, which I wore at the ripe old age of 19, was all of those things. Now it is in my basement storage! A few months ago I put it on again. I even got it zipped, which made me really proud. Even though I looked like a middle aged woman in a wedding gown, I felt beautiful, like I was a pure, beautiful young bride.

As we explore this next section of Galatians, we are going to talk about wedding clothes. These clothes are our spiritual wedding

gown, which is truly beautiful, magical and perfect. It is profoundly costly and deeply more than just symbolic.

I'm excited to study this section of scripture, for those very reasons above. When I remember what, or more specifically, with whom I am clothed, I know I am his beautiful, pure bride.

We already know from the previous study of Galatians 3, that we are sons and daughters of Abraham. We know that we were made part of the family of faith and made heirs of the irrevocable promise given to Father Abraham. We also know that God planned for us when he made that promise to Abraham. We know that Jesus, as he alone could, fulfilled the terms of the other promise, made through the law of Moses and in doing so, released us from being bound by it. Those facts are all worth being excited about! But what we read in Galatians 3:26-29 should send us over the top! Let's read it now.

1. Whose sons (and daughters) are we according to verse 26?

2. Reread verses 28 and 29. Why do you think that it is important for Paul to remind them of this?

3. In verse 29, what do you read as the key or way to being included in the promise made to Abraham?

So, we know that it is being "in Christ" that adds us to God's family. This is what makes us his sons and daughters. We are

heirs of the greater promise. The one that is given and kept by God alone. When we try to follow the rules, or in the case of the Galatian believers, the law of Moses, we are submitting to a promise that depends on our ability to keep it to perfection in order for it to be binding. We know that we cannot do it! Why depend on the inferior promise? Why try to perform our way up the ladder to acceptance and worth in the King's household when we are already his sons and daughters?

These verses are a beautiful reminder that we are in fact children of God, not by what we have done, are doing, or will do, but based only on what Jesus, himself, already did. It seems crazy to think that we are valued by God and given position based on our own goodness and actions, but I find myself struggling with that mindset in one form or another. Sometimes, I think my worth to God is about whether I'm a "good girl," who does the right thing and follows the rules. Sometimes I think it is about how completely I fill out my Bible study, or whether I'm a "good" wife or mom. The Bible tells me, however what my "good" works or actions are worth if I'm depending on them to make me good enough for God.

Look at Isaiah 64:6 (NIV)
> All of us have become like one who is unclean,
> and all our righteous acts are like filthy rags;
> we all shrivel up like a leaf,
> and like the wind our sins sweep us away.

4.   To what does this verse compare our personal acts, or works, of righteousness?

I looked up the word "filthy" in Strong's Concordance for the Hebrew meaning. I was planning on including this definition in this study, but it was actually too graphic for my comfort! Obviously, God chose this word so I'm not saying it's too graphic

in general. I just couldn't bring myself to include the actual definition. Let me just tell you that it involves the feminine hygiene aisle at the grocery store. Moving back into my comfort zone, I will share that my youngest son wore cloth diapers for over a year, and the words "filthy rags" brought these to mind. Anyway, you get the point. What we do in order to be good, or "righteous acts," are like soiled rags. They are not clean enough nor suitable enough to clothe us. We are NOT adequately or even decently covered by them. I think you could further argue that if we tried to be clothed by our own acts of righteousness, we'd stink!

I can't help but notice that we are about as far away from the wedding dress in the opening of this day's study as we could possibly be! So, where does the beautiful white gown come in? Let's take a look again at the section of Galatians we are studying today, specifically, verse, 27.

5. What does this verse say we "put on" when we are baptized into Christ?

That is awesome and beautiful, isn't it? He is awesome and beautiful. We know our nakedness is exposed when we sin. We know that we, like Adam and Eve, have tried to cover ourselves by our own power, and in doing so, try to be made right or righteous again. We also know that our own efforts are like trying to wear dirty diapers on the red carpet. But, here we read about the garment that God planned and willed for us to wear! We put on Jesus. He covers us in the robes of righteousness.

Before we wrap up Galatians 3, let's look at a couple of additional scriptures that talk about the nature of what we wear when we put on Christ. Let's take our minds back to that wedding dress, the beautiful garment that represents purity and we will end there. I have kids and a dog, I come in contact with plenty of filthy rags through the course of a day. I'm thrilled to end this day

encouraged that not only is that not what I'm trying to cover myself with but that Jesus has clothed me in beauty and purity!

6. Read Isaiah 61:10. What do you read about the garment God provides?

7. Read Matthew 22:1-14. (This is a parable, which is a simple story used to illustrate a moral lesson. Keep in mind that you may not be able to ascribe deep and specific meaning to each word of the parable)

   a. Who do you think could be represented by verse 8?

   b. Who could be represented in verse 9?

   c. What was a guest missing in verse 11?

   d. What happened to the man who did not wear the wedding clothes?

   e. What do you think could be represented by the wedding clothes?

f.   In regards to our relationship with God, how do we get the wedding clothes?

What a beautiful image! We put on Christ! We are no longer trying to cover ourselves in filthy rags. The robes of righteousness, which are given to us, are like a wedding dress, in that they were very costly. Jesus paid for them. These costly clothes don't just represent purity; they cover us in it! They unite us to a groom who loves us with all he is, and he brings us into his royal family.

As we come to the very close of Galatians chapter 3, we read that because of the one with whom we have been united in baptism and with whom we have been clothed, we are now all equal. This isn't an equality in lowness and failure, this is a beautiful equality. We are all children in the holy family. That idea is so far above how we try to compare! If we continue thinking about how we establish worth through our achievements in the light of the filthy rags of our own work, it becomes clear how ridiculous this is. Who would think to see who is the best or who is worth more by comparing which dirty diaper is the least nasty? No one! Put on Jesus! Remember what we wore and who we were without him! Remember that our beauty, purity, our very rightness with God is a gift, the robes of righteousness, given by Jesus. Remember that our brothers and sisters in Jesus are clothed with him too. There are no bests, no worsts. We are all at the banquet because we wear the righteousness he has given us!

The Point:

All who have "put on" Jesus are now sons and daughters of God. We do not achieve this by what we do, and therefore our right standing is not of our own work. Our brothers and sisters are just like us. They are not less, worse, more or better. We are all covered by Jesus.

The Questions:

1. Have you been baptized in and are you being continually immersed into Christ? Explain.

2. How do you feel knowing that you are clothed with Jesus?

3. Are there times when you have tried to be pure and beautiful but you were actually covered in filthy rags? Explain.

4. In the parable that we read in Matthew 22, who ultimately attended the banquet? Is it likely that they had their own wedding clothes when they were invited? Where do you think they got them?

5. How does it affect the way you view others who have accepted Jesus as their savior, knowing that there is no distinction (Jew nor Greek, Slave nor Free, Male nor Female)?

TO BE KNOWN

Read Galatians 4:1-11

I recently watched my first episode of the show "Fixer Upper." The show is about an adorable young couple who fix up disastrous houses for their clients. The couple, Chip and Joanna Gaines, are parents to four young kids. The family is delightful to watch. On the episode I watched, Chip casually mentioned that he was planning to take the kids to the animal shelter to "look at" a kitten. After some back and forth banter, but no forthcoming revelation from Chip, Joanna reminded him that they had a cat. She also sternly encouraged him not to get another cat or a dog. After Chip left the room, the cameras were on Joanna alone and she quipped, "he's going to get a dog. "

When Chip returned later in the episode, he had not one, but two kittens and he told Joanna that they had also gotten a dog. She just chuckled. She wasn't surprised. She knew it. She knew him.

This exchange is why I found them delightful. I thought, "she knows him, and she loves him."

It's a beautiful thing to be known. We yearn for it. We want others to know us down deep and still love us. Sometimes I find myself blurting out the stuff that might prevent people from fully loving me, just to force them to know something about me and deal with it! You know, something like, "I didn't get a chance to shower today!" After it's out there, then I'm thinking, "Ok, they know. Now will they love me?"

The truth is, I am both fully known and fully loved. So are you. We are going to study this very idea in our next section of Galatians. The idea of being fully known and fully loved is so lovely and so secure.

At the end of Galatians Chapter 3, we were reminded that not only are we heirs to promises of God, we are his children. We donned our beautiful robes of righteousness and we are clothed with Christ. We learned that we are children of God and we are all equal in his family. Now Paul begins to explain our place in God's family. Read Galatians 4:1-7.

1. Using very simple terms, rewrite Galatians 4:1-3 in your own words.

Here is a paraphrase of these verses from *The Message*:
"Let me show you the implications of this. As long as the heir is a minor, he has no advantage over the slave. Though legally he owns the entire inheritance, he is subject to tutors and administrators until whatever date the father has set for emancipation. That is the way it is with us: When we were minors, we were just like slaves ordered around by simple instructions (the tutors and administrators of this world), with no say in the conduct of our own lives."

Now read Galatians 4:4-7.

  2.   What is the first word in verse 4?

Verse 4 starts out with the word "but." That's an awesome word right here in the Bible! It tells us that reality was a certain imperfect way, and then God steps in and makes it perfect and right. In this case, those in God's family were in fact sons, but they were under authority with no more freedom than a slave. But. This means it's all about to change!

  3.   What do you learn happened from verses 4-5?

  4.   What change does this bring to our status in the family of God?

  5.   Who is sent to us?

  6.   Where is he sent?

  7.   What does it say he does in these verses?

What a picture of intimacy. These verses start out reminding the Galatians and us of our family history. God's people were once like children, subject to the rules. They had status, but no rights as heirs. They had no freedom. But... We read in verse 4 that God sent Jesus to redeem those children and give them full rights as sons.

In questions 5-7 above, we studied what Paul, the Galatians, and we, receive as sons (and daughters). We receive the Spirit of Jesus, who resides in our hearts and calls out "daddy." I find these words so interesting. I love that the Spirit does this work of intimacy for us. I know, for example, that it is true that I love and trust God. I also know that I neither do this perfectly nor fully. In fact, I have never seen God and I do not fully know him. I know some about his nature and I know some of the wonderful and good things he has done for me. All this being said, I still find it hard to totally connect with the idea that he is "daddy." Who better to connect me to God as "daddy" than his firstborn son Jesus? I can't think of a better way for Jesus to make this connection for me than through his Spirit, living right in my heart! his Spirit intimately connects me with God, my "daddy."

In verse 9 we read even more about our intimate connection.

8. What does verse 9 say about our connection with God and his with us?

This really stands out to me. Not only does Jesus' Spirit within us connect us to God, God is connected to us. We read that we are known by him. That is so hard for me to comprehend because I also know that he loves me. How comforting, safe and beautiful to be fully known and yet loved by him. This is the relationship that

He made possible through Jesus. This is the freedom and realization as child of God that Paul is talking about.

We've read Paul talk about two different paths in pursuit of God in chapters 3 and 4 of Galatians. One is the path of being a child of God, heir to his unconditional promise, redeemed by Jesus and given his Spirit who cries out "daddy" from the very interior of our souls. The other is the path of submission to that which we cannot live out perfectly. The path of slavery. One path leads to life and is a faithful dependence on Jesus. The other leads to death and is a dependence on our own abilities or on the rules and approval of others.

Paul reminds the Galatians of the path to death in the last few verses we are studying today. Read Galatians 4:8-11.

9.   How many times do you see the word, or form of the word "slave"?

10.   To whom or what were they enslaved?

11.   What adjectives are used to describe the principles to which they submit in verse 9?

I'm struck by the complete contrast in verse 9. This is the same verse where we learned that the Galatians were known by God. In the last half of the verse we see they are submitting to something far below God. Something that has no power and brings no joy. As

I think about this contrast, I've been dwelling on the idea that the Galatians were going to submit to something. They could submit to their position as sons in the family of God, the God who intimately knows them and to whom the Spirit calls out "daddy." Conversely, they could submit to those who are by nature not gods. They could submit to something weak and miserable. The right, best, healthy choice seems clear!

The Point:

We are free sons of God. We have been redeemed from slavery by Jesus and then given his Spirit. His Spirit dwells in our hearts and causes our hearts to connect to him and call out to our God, our "daddy."

The Questions:

1. What are rules and laws to which you find yourself "subject?" What would bring freedom?

2. What does it mean to have an intimate connection and relationship with the Father?

3. How does it encourage you in your relationship with God through his word (Bible) and in prayer to know that the Spirit is making an intimate connection for you?

4. Do you wish to be seen and known fully by someone? How would you feel if you are fully seen and known, and still loved unconditionally? Even more, loved to the point that a sacrifice is made to be with you?

5. Based on what we've studied in Galatians, why would Paul be so offended that the Galatians were depending on teachers of the Jewish law and following the Jewish law in order to be right with God?

6.   What is the likelihood of being fully realized, or actualized, if you submit to something or someone who is by nature *not* god?

7.   Can freedom and submission coexist?

8.   Explain how being known by God and living in submission to him leads to freedom.

9.   Now, go get that puppy!

PERPLEXING

Read Galatians 4:12-20

Childbirth is painful. I doubt there is much to debate on that topic. It hurts. I have experienced it twice, giving birth to two children. I don't think there is a single person who would want to go through the process and pain of child birth two times for the same child! When you are trying to deliver anything into life, it is hard work and a painful process. No one would want to repeat that work and pain only to start in the place where they were before. Paul actually uses the analogy of going through childbirth a second time to describe what he is going through for the Galatians. Paul says he's perplexed. I've got to say, I would find that perplexing as well! What is going on here that has pushed these Galatians back into the womb? Let's study and find out.

1. Read Galatians 4:12-16. List words or phrases from these verses that describe how Paul was treated by the Galatians when he was first with them.

2.   How is he being treated in verse 16? Why?

3.   According to verse 15, what do the Galatians seem to be missing?

It's hard to understand how the Galatians could go from treating Paul with such care and honor to considering him an enemy. No wonder Paul is perplexed!

I also find it perplexing that a group of people would go through all the effort to infiltrate this church and "bewitch" them into following the Jewish law. I've been really trying to figure out why they would do this. The next few verses we will study provide some insight into this question. Read Galatians 4:17-20.

4.   What do you read about the motivation of those trying to win over the Galatians?

5.   Why were they trying to alienate the Galatians from Paul?

Now we know something about the motivation of those trying to win over the Galatians. They want glory for themselves. They want people to be excited, and even more so, zealous for them. Paul on the other hand, had no interest in having glory for himself.

In the Gospel of John, Jesus gives us a picture of those pursuing personal glory. Read John 7:14-19.

6.   What does this scripture say a person does in order to gain honor for themselves?

7.   How does Jesus describe a person who works for the honor of the "one who sent him?"

8.   How are these descriptions consistent with Paul and his teaching and with the Judaizers and their teaching from Galatians?

As I've been studying this section of Galatians, I've been thinking about this issue of "glory." It is as if it is a litmus test, of sorts, for truth. In our culture, we encounter very persuasive teachers and arguments, making it difficult to really identify the truth. Obviously, we, unlike the Galatians, have the full word of God in the Bible. God's word is, no doubt, a solid and reliable test by which to understand and recognize truth. Another test, though, can certainly be identifying who gets the glory. If there is a teacher who is seeking honor and glory for himself, you can know that he is speaking on his own and for his own purposes. If there is one

who speaks from God and to God be the glory, just as scripture says, this is a person of truth.

While I think this "glory" test is worthwhile in applying to the teaching of others, the most telling place for this test is in my own life and behavior. I should ask myself, "who gets the glory?" before I act, teach, share... I want to be a woman of truth. I want to be able to discern truth. I don't want to be perplexing or cause double labor pains in order for God to bring life to me!

The Point:

When we try to earn our righteousness, it is only ever for our glory. When we share our beliefs to make converts to our way, it is only ever for our glory. A woman of truth seeks to bring glory to God.

The Questions:

1. Paul became free by not submitting to the law to be righteous, but rather to Jesus. Do you surrender to Jesus for freedom, or are you still trying to control it by following rules?

2. The Galatians were very good at actions of goodness, until their motives were exposed. If they were doing it to be good, they felt good, unless the wrong was pointed out and then they treated Paul as an enemy. Is this selfless or selfish?

3. How do you respond when someone who loves you points out your wrong actions?

4. How do you know if you are acting as a woman of truth?

SLAVE OR FREE?

Read Galatians 4:21-31

A few chapters ago, I mentioned that Paul had shared a figurative story in order to explain to the Galatians the difference between following the law of Moses and depending, in faith, on Jesus for salvation. Well, here it is. Let's spend some time studying this example Paul gave us as we close the study in this issue.

Read Galatians 4:21-31.

1. Name the two women and their children Paul mentioned in these verses.

2. List details about each that Paul shares with the Galatians.

3.   What does Paul say each woman/child represent?

Read Hebrews 11:8-11 (ESV)
8 By faith Abraham obeyed when he was called to go out to a place that he was to receive as an inheritance. And he went out, not knowing where he was going. 9 By faith he went to live in the land of promise, as in a foreign land, living in tents with Isaac and Jacob, heirs with him of the same promise. 10 For he was looking forward to the city that has foundations, whose designer and builder is God. 11 By faith Sarah herself received power to conceive, even when she was past the age, since she considered him faithful who had promised.

4.   What connections do you see between Hebrews 11:10 and Galatians 4:26-28?

5.   What happened with each child in Galatians 4:30?

We are going to spend the rest of this study time reading in Genesis, so I'm keeping the reading here short. Take some time and read Genesis 12-22. Pay particular attention to Abraham (Abram), Sarah (Sarai), Hagar, Ishmael and Isaac.

6. List facts about Ishmael, his birth parents, the circumstances surrounding his conception and birth order.

7. List facts about Isaac, his birth parents, the circumstances surrounding his conception and birth order.

8. Based on what you know, what could have been some things Ishmael used to "mock" Isaac?

The Point:

Salvation comes only through the promise God made, not through following the law.

The Questions:

1. Write down modern day examples of how people try to achieve righteousness by following the rules.

2. How can we really be credited with righteousness today?

3. How might a legalist today mock someone who is free?

4. Are you perfect? Does it matter? If you aren't perfect, are you enough without Jesus' gift, to be good?

5. Ponder the temporal or eternal nature of the two promises.

6. Explain whether you are living as a child of the slave woman or of the free?

THAT DOESN'T COUNT!

Read Galatians 5:1-6

My youngest boy just got a new game, called "Pop the Pig." It's pretty awesome and very funny. The game consists of a very porky pig, dressed in a chef's hat, holding a spatula. He's wearing a little set of trousers with a belt that buckles, and a little scarf around his neck, as if he's a French food critic. In addition, the game has 4 sets of small colored pieces, shaped like hamburgers, in green, red, purple and yellow. Each color set's burger has a number on the bottom from 1 to 4. The game comes with a die that has colored sides to coordinate with the colors on the burgers. The burgers go into the pig's mouth, and you press down on the pig's head a corresponding number of times as the number on the bottom of the burger that you choose based on the roll of the die. Each time you push the pig's head, his belly grows just a little, until finally, it gets so big his belt pops open and his arms fly up. You've just popped the pig!

When Bennett got the game, he wanted to play it right away, so he enlisted the help of his teenaged brother. Since there aren't many parts to the game and it appears pretty straight forward, the boys just pulled it out and started playing without reading the instructions. In their game, the person who caused the pig to pop, was the loser.

When my husband got home from work, he was immediately recruited to play. Since he had never seen the game, and having more patience and self-control than either our preschooler or teenager, he read the instructions! Guess what. According to the instructions, the person to pop the pig is actually the winner! All those losses DIDN'T COUNT. What do I mean? I mean they won't go down in the record book. They weren't truly losses. They didn't matter. I also mean that Bennett felt simultaneously ticked off and vindicated. He knew he wasn't the loser. The games didn't count.

We want to know what matters; what counts. We care about doing those things that really mean something. Who wants to spend time messing with stuff that doesn't count? It seems meaningless.

In Galatians chapter 5, Paul speaks to his readers in terms of what really counts. I was pretty excited to read it! I want to invest in what counts. I don't want to "pop the pig" to no avail! As we read and study the first 6 verses of Galatians 5, we are going to look at what Paul says is the only thing that "counts."

Paul spent the bulk of his letter to the Galatians reminding them that they are free from following the law. What's more, he reminded them that they cannot perfectly obey the law. He told them that they are not under obligation or slavery to the law, but rather, the law was fulfilled by Jesus, in whom they put their faith. It is as a result of this faith, or dependence, adherence, reliance upon, Jesus that they are "credited" with righteousness.

As we pick up our study in Galatians 5:1 we learn the result of Jesus' free gift. Read Galatians 5:1-6.

1.   According to Galatians 5:1, what is the goal or result of being set free by Jesus?

2.   What are they to stand firm against?

It is interesting that Paul tells them to "stand firm." This implies that it is not easy to rest in freedom, but more common to depend on following certain rules to ensure we are "good enough."

3.   Do you find this to be a struggle personally? If so, how do you stand firm in the truth that Jesus has fulfilled the rules for you and has given you the gift of freedom?

Paul gives them a very definitive and serious warning in verse 2. He repeats it in verse 3.

4.   What does Paul say the result will be if the Galatians submit to circumcision?

Those are incredibly strong words. He doesn't talk in passive terms like: "if you do this, such and such *could* happen." Paul says if they submit to or depend on following the law in order to be right with God, "Christ will be of no value." Furthermore, he says in verse 4:

"You are severed from Christ, you who would be justified by the law; you have fallen away from grace." ESV

In these verses, Paul is not talking about being so sinful there is not enough room for the free gift of Jesus grace in our lives. Paul is saying that when we try to earn righteousness, by being perfectly obedient and believing that this is a way to be with God, we are no longer connected with Jesus and his grace.

Before we get to the verse where Paul tells the Galatians what really counts, we have to take a deeper look at verse 5. This verse is such a beautiful statement of what faith and righteousness really "look like." The Galatian believers were being pressured into taking action that would be a visible display of what they must do or connect with to be righteous. They were being pressured to be circumcised, an outward sign that they were "doing right to be right." In verse 5, Paul reminds them that the righteous wait and hope, through the power of the Holy Spirit in what Jesus has already done. Weird, right? At the very least, it seems counter intuitive and counter cultural to me. When I think about belonging to a group or family, I'm reminded that many groups have outward, visible evidence of membership. In Scouts, you wear a uniform and a badge. In other organizations, you might wear a certain color of hat or a pin on your shirt. What Paul is calling a marker of being a part of the family of those made right with God is waiting in faith. What for? Read Galatians 5:5-6

5.   What does Paul eagerly wait for?

The righteous are the ones hopefully waiting for what God has done, not the ones cutting away flesh and following the rules.

So what counts then? What is it that sets those in the family of God apart? We just read verse 6, so it's clear that it is not circumcision, which for us would represent doing right to be right, or following the rules, even what we consider rules in the Bible.

6. Finish Galatians 5:6 "For in Christ Jesus neither circumcision nor uncircumcision counts for anything, but only _____. "(ESV) ·

There we have it! What "counts" or really matters of those following Jesus is "faith working through love." Mmm. Mmm. This is about to get good! Let's look at some scripture that tells us what love looks like. Wait! You might ask, "Aren't we just about to study how to act to be right?" It's true that we are going to look at some specific actions that are characteristics of Biblical love. Followers of Jesus, however, aren't acting with love to be right. Rather, they are acting with love in hope. It's the hope from verse 5! Hope in what Jesus has already done for us to be right! Hope that love shown by action is grounded in who we are eternally, and not what we want and expect in return. Let's look at some specific things Paul, writing in the Spirit of God, says about what love, carried out in faith, looks like.

7. Read 1 Corinthians 13. Based on verses 4-8 what are some specific characteristics of love?

8. Read Romans 12:9-21. What are specific characteristics of love listed in these verses?

9. Read Romans 13:8-11. What does love look like according to these verses?

10.   What is the nature of acts of love based on 1 Corinthians 13:8?

11.   What does Romans 13:8 say about those who love one another?

Those 13:8s are good aren't they! Romans 13:8 is pretty interesting in light of what we are studying in Galatians. Here are the Galatians, struggling. They are being told and deceived into believing that they can be saved or right with God, by following the law. Paul reminds them that they are saved by Jesus, the fulfillment of the law. How did he fulfill the law? He loved perfectly! Love. That is how the law is fulfilled! Love, carried out in faith in the hope of who Jesus has made us. That is how the law is fulfilled. Isn't that freeing?

* * *

The Point:

We are burdened by rules. We are liberated by Jesus. He set us free so that we could be free and when we try to follow rules instead of Jesus, we are living as if we think we can do it without him. It doesn't matter if we look like we are living by the rules or not, what truly matters is that we have faith in Jesus and we show it by the way we love.

The Questions:

1. Explain "for freedom you were set free" in your own words.

2. Name some places where you feel that you are not free. Are there rules you are following to attain freedom?

3. Why do you think Paul encourages the Galatians to "stand firm?"

4. What "counts" or matters in Jesus?

5. What is the basis of expressing love?

6. Are you trying to work your way up the ladder of goodness? Explain. Is this true freedom?

7. How have you accepted the GIFT of grace by putting faith in Jesus' love and not your own goodness or actions?

8. How do you wait for the gift of righteousness? With anticipation and longing or by trying to work for it?

9. How are you affected by the idea that expressions of love are what "counts?"

10. After reading about love, what have you learned about faith and love? Is it based on feeling or an active work?

HE CUT ME OFF

Read Galatians 5:7-15

My kids got a new video game for Christmas. It is an animated car racing game. Remember Mario? Well, now apparently, he's a great car racer! Sadly, I'm not! Hopefully, this is a commentary on my video gaming skills and not my driving skills. When discussing my gaming skills, my older son told his friend that I can't even jump in the Lego video games. This, believe it or not, is a big criticism in teenaged gaming terms! In the Mario racing game, there is more than just driving. You can sabotage other players by bumping into them, throwing ink on their screen, and dropping banana peels on the track; all virtually, of course. If I was ever to be a victor in this game, I would need to be the only car on the track!

One time, in playing with my 5-year-old, I was actually in first place. I was running a good race. Sadly, it was short lived. Although, at one point, I was bound for a victorious finish,

Bennett sabotaged me! He cut me off. Needless to say, I didn't win.

Paul uses these terms with his Galatian readers, well, minus the gaming references. In Galatians 5:7 he tells them they were running a good race but that they had been cut off. The idea of the Galatians being cut off from their victory is much more significant than my loss at Mario Cart! The victory for which they were headed is eternal and full righteousness. This is certainly not something from which anyone would want to be cut off! In the next few verses, Paul clearly states what he thinks about those trying to lead the Galatians down the wrong path, and then Paul effectively "cuts off" any more talk of them until the end of his letter.

In verses 7-12, Paul concludes most of his discussion about the Judaizers.

1. Read Galatians 5:7-12. What consequence for the Judaizers does Paul have confidence in?

2. According to verse 11, what do the Judaizers avoid? What does Paul experience?

3. What word does Paul use to describe the work at the cross in verse 11?

4. What does "offense" or "stumbling block" mean? Why is the cross offensive?

5. How did the Judaizers, who taught that that followers of Jesus must obey the law, remove or abolish the offense of the cross?

Total dependence on anything other than ourselves is completely foreign, isn't it? Even my 5-year-old is passionate about doing it all himself! This morning on the way to preschool, he informed me that he could drive; an idea probably reinforced by the beat down he gave me on the racing video game! When we got to school, he insisted on walking himself down the hall, up the stairs, down the other hall, and into his class. It is human nature to want to control our destiny, actions and even our day. We would rather have a system that depends on our own abilities to effect our personal salvation. We can understand it. Yet, here, we are called to submit to the "offense" of the cross. Only Jesus can save; there is nothing we can do to bring about our own righteousness. We must be dependent, not independent.

As we read on from verse 11 to verse 12, although according to the NIV Study Bible Notes, Paul is employing a bit of sarcasm, he also gives a very clear picture of our efforts be righteous on our own. Read Galatians 5:12. Paul says he wishes those advocating circumcision would go ahead and emasculate themselves. The result of that action is impotence! No life could be effected. Isn't it interesting that Paul would say this. An act such as this would be a visible sign of impotence for these false teachers who were calling for others to be circumcised, a visible sign of following the law, in an effort to become righteous. If the Judaizers, Galatians or believers in God today try to follow all the right rules, relying on their own ability to be saved, the result is the same as those who were teaching and depending on circumcision. Failure.

Impotence. No potential for life. These ideas go against our grain, don't they! Self-reliance and independence equal impotence and failure. Total dependence, on Jesus, equals righteousness, potency (life) and ultimately, perfection.

After Paul calls for the Judaizers to cut themselves off, that is essentially what he does. Paul shifts his writing from the error of the Judaizers to the freedom and life found by believers in Jesus. He reminds them of their freedom. Read Galatians 5:13-15.

6.   What caution does Paul give the Galatians in verse 13?

7.   Can you think of examples today where our culture uses freedom to "indulge the flesh?"

8.   What does verse 13 say we can use freedom for?

9.   Read verse 14-15. Paul says the "entire law is fulfilled in keeping this one command." What is it? Use your Bible cross reference to find and record this idea confirmed elsewhere in Scripture.

10.   What is the caveat Paul gives in verse 15 and what would be the result of engaging in this behavior?

That's so cool! The Galatian believers have been pressured, confused and misled that they must follow the entire Jewish law in order to be saved, righteous, and victorious. Now, after telling them that Jesus has given them freedom from following these rules, Paul tells them how in their freedom they can fulfill the law! Of course, this isn't easy and no one can do it perfectly, but the freedom rests in the fact that Jesus has already done it perfectly! The Galatians, and us, for that matter, are free to join Jesus in participating. Knowing that even in our imperfection, we are racing toward victory in Jesus!

Yes, being dependent is scandalous and offensive, but being so gives us freedom, victory and love. Jesus is worth the scandal! He certainly thought we were. Let's depend on him.

The Point:

Freedom comes only from Jesus, not from following rules. Freedom isn't about taking advantage of Jesus' gift of righteousness to live however we please. Nor is it about trying force others to live by the rules we think are required to be free. Freedom is about love. A dependent love that brings about life and potency.

The Questions:

1. What were the Galatians cut off from in vs 7?

2. How did Paul feel about those teaching circumcision?

3. Explain in your own words what Paul meant in verse 11 about the offense of the cross.

4. What sums up the entire law?

5. Do you, like Paul, feel passionate about the freedom that is in faith in Jesus? If so, how do you share that with others?

6. How do you share the truth?

7. Are you willing to share, knowing that the truth is a stumbling block or offensive?

8. How do you live in your freedom? What do you gratify? Flesh or love?

9. Do you set yourself up for failure in trying to be right by following the law? Explain. How can you actually fulfill the law?

10. What outward sign was important to the Judaizers that represented their submission to the law?

11. What seal of success or sign has God given us? (See Ephesians 1:13)

FLESH OR FRUIT: GRATIFICATION OR GROWTH?

Read Galatians 5:16-26

Have you ever watched The Biggest Loser? I just watched an episode for the first time. The episode I watched is all about temptation. The very first challenge the contestants faced was to choose between a big sum of money or continuing on the show. It was a hard temptation. Basically, they could have chosen between feeding their desire for money, which each contestant admitted wouldn't last, or between staying and growing in their abilities to live a healthy lifestyle. If they took the money, they had to go home. They could not stay to learn and grow. I have to admit, it was so intense, that I didn't make it through the whole episode in one sitting. (I also kept crying right along with the contestants, so I turned it off so my teenager wouldn't have more reasons to laugh at me!)

What I saw, reminded me of the principles in Galatians 5:16-26. The similar concepts I saw included the choice between feeding something unhealthy and destructive, or refusing to feed the craving, and choosing to live a new way and experience personal growth. They were opposing forces. Growth just wasn't going to come from feeding the desire to eat and eat badly. Growth was going to come by walking in a new way. Sitting at home and watching from the comfort of my comfort zone, it was easy to see which choice contestants should make. It was obvious which decision would constitute a poor choice. Sitting back and watching, I could yell out, "don't do it!"

Shifting focus from the reality show, to the reality that the Galatians experienced, let's look at the opposing forces Paul talks about in Galatians 5:16-26. Let's explore the cravings that Paul warns them, and us, not to feed and the path and results of not doing so.

In our last lesson, we studied what Paul said truly fulfills the law. You'll remember that it is in fact, love. We also studied what love looks like. We know love looks like Jesus. The word made flesh. He is the incarnation of love. We briefly studied the Holy Spirit, the seal of our faith. The Spirit of our Lord Jesus, is where we are fueled and powered to love. Now, as we study this section of Galatians, Paul is going to help the Galatians and us understand what we look like, or what the growth from us in the Spirit is like.

Read Galatians 5:16-18

1. What does Paul say is to be the Galatians' active relationship with the Spirit? (What does he tell them to do in regards to the Spirit?)

2. From verse 16, what is the result of the above?

3.   Look up the word "flesh" in a dictionary and write down the definition which you think applies here.

4.   What word summarizes the relationship between the Spirit and the flesh?

Read Galatians 5:19-21. Paul says that what comes from feeding the craving, or the flesh, is evident and obvious. This is so interesting to me. I don't think Paul is giving the Galatians a list to use in order to judge the rightness of other people. When we think about these "works of the flesh," it is obvious, isn't it? These actions do not in any way describe God. It's so obvious that these are works of the flesh, that a fiction writer wouldn't even use these actions to describe a human protagonist. It's clear that these actions are without virtue; just as clear as whether or not a contestant on the Biggest Loser should eat junk food!

5.   List the works of the flesh.

Now, before we get too comfortable in our own exemption from these sins, or our own goodness, let's remember that Paul warns us not to feed the craving. In fact, Paul reminds us in Galatians over and over again that righteousness is through faith and not through following the rules. When we try to achieve perfection by following rules we will fail. In knowing this, it's clear that we are not perfect, and therefore not innocent of every sin on this list!

The idea of craving implies that we hunger for something. We may experience a desire or hunger to feed one of these acts. We are not innocent. As I survey this list of acts of the flesh, I think about how easy it is to feed a craving. How about feeding division by making one small passive aggressive statement to fuel a divisive conversation? What about feeding dissension by complaining about the speaker at church, or the manner in which the worship team leads songs? Also, I see verse 21 as a very stern warning about "gratifying" those desires.

6. Look up the word "gratify." Write the definition.

7. How would gratifying a desire be different from being a sinner but not walking "by the Spirit" as Paul encouraged the Galatians to do?

If we are believers in Jesus, we have the Holy Spirit! We can "stay in step" with him. We have blessed assurance of our destiny. I believe this section of scripture, and this is me talking here, is to tell the Galatians and us: "hey, this stuff is obvious." "If someone is living and investing like this, they are living to satisfy their flesh. They aren't living like a person with the Spirit. This is common sense. You can tell evil from good!"

Having said that, let's actually take some time to focus on what God through his Spirit wants to cultivate for believers in whom his Spirit lives. This is the good stuff!

Read Galatians 5:22-23

8. Paul calls this list the "_____ of the Spirit."

9.   List the 9 fruits of the Spirit Paul shares here.

10. List some things you know about literal fruit.

11. Take some time to think of a few comparisons between literal and spiritual fruit. Write them down. I'll start with an example:

Fruit has seeds that when planted are the catalyst for new life and growth. God's fruit in me can produce seeds that are planted in my children and spiritual children.

This is some seriously sweet fruit! I love that Paul contrasts feeding a craving, a sinful desire, with receiving fruit from God. What better way to feed our growth in relationship with Jesus than to feed us with good, healthy, sweetness!

When Wesley, my teenager, was little, I used to tell him that these fruits were our real super powers! He, like most boys, has always been into super heroes. Can you imagine a hero with the power of God to act in love, joy, peace, patience, kindness, goodness, faithfulness, gentleness and self-control? Pretty awesome and beautiful, huh? And to think, these fruits are ours. These are the actions and qualities God grows in our lives when we are in step

with his Spirit. He gives all of them. Some may be in the form of a seed right now, but others may be a big ripe fruit!

Before we finish today's lesson, let's take a closer look at verse 24. Read this verse now.

12.   What does this verse say of those who belong to Jesus?

Even though the acts of the flesh and the fruit of the Spirit are obvious, living by the Spirit isn't necessarily described as easy. Paul says those "who belong to Jesus have crucified the flesh with its passions and desires." (ESV) Crucifixion is in no way considered a simple, painless death. The use of this term both connects the believers with what Jesus has already done and what his Spirit does in us. Putting our flesh or nature to death could be slow and painful! Take heart in knowing, however that we know the outcome!

Read Philippians 1:6-11.

13.   What does Philippians 1:6 say God will do?

14.   Based on verse 6, how confident of this outcome can we be?

Read 1 John 3:1-3

15.   Based on verse 2, what will believers experience when Jesus appears?

We have hope, don't we! We know one day all of the fruit of the Spirit will be perfectly ripe in us. How encouraging! How beautiful! One day we will be completely full, perfect in love, joy, peace, patience, kindness, goodness, faithfulness, gentleness and self-control! It's guaranteed!

The Point:

Believers are to live freely by the Spirit. When we do, we won't fill up our sinful desires but our lives experience growth. The growth of valuable virtues, such as love, joy, peace, patience, kindness, goodness, faithfulness, gentleness and self-control.

The Questions:

1. What are the results of feeding something?

2. What does the idea that the passions and desires of the sinful nature must be crucified imply? (vs 24)?

3. Would crucifixion be a quick and easy event or a long and difficult one?

4. Are there acts of the flesh in your life? Do you feed them? How?

5. Who is responsible for fruit in your life?

6. What verbs do you find in these verses regarding our participation with the Spirit?

7. Are you feeding a craving or exercising by walking?

WE ARE A BODY

Read Galatians 6:1-10

This past summer, I took an epic girl's trip! I met my girlfriends in California and we traveled to Yosemite National Park. We were all celebrating birthdays. Our choice of celebration wasn't eating cake and ice cream. We chose to climb Half Dome, one of the iconic monoliths in Yosemite. It was hard on all of us, but we made it! I felt a huge sense of accomplishment. I was proud that I was able to make the hike without holding my friends up. I also felt like I was finally back in action, physically! I felt in shape and confident.

Two days after getting home, I had some free time in Rocky Mountain National Park. Both of my boys were in a day long camp nearby, so I figured I would enjoy my renewed physical confidence and hike while the kiddos were in camp. About 8 miles into the 11 miles of hiking I had planned for the day, I slipped and fell and twisted my ankle. I heard my ankle snap as I went down! It was gross. My ankle immediately swelled to elephant size, and

in direct proportion to the amount my confidence shrunk! It was a total bummer to say the least and even 7 months later, my injured ankle is still not the same size as the healthy one!

Although I didn't break my ankle, I tore up some stuff in there (this is my technical medical assessment of the situation!) It was quite a while before I actually walked normally. The good news is; it was not quite a while before I could walk. In fact, we live in a two-story house. Our laundry room is on the main floor and our bedrooms are on the second floor. Exactly two sections of eight steps each, divided by a landing. I count them because I'm generally clumsy and I'm not interested in falling again any time soon. Basically, all that tells you that it was imperative that my body find a way upstairs. And so I did. It wasn't pretty, and it sure wasn't perfect, but it worked! I hobbled up and down those stairs and around my house countless times.

The point is, the rest of my body was fine, and in fact, healthy. Because of this, my right leg helped out. It helped carry the slack from my left ankle to allow time for it not to bear as much weight, not feel as much pain and to heal. Our bodies are amazing that way. It is no wonder that God used our understanding of our body and its ability to compensate, function and recover to teach us something about our relationships with each other in Jesus. (Hopefully that's what I'm getting at; and I'm not just hyper focused on sharing injury and pain!)

We are going to get a glimpse of what the body of Christ looks like from Paul's next words to the Galatians. He doesn't specifically use the term "body" in this passage, although he does in other passages. (See: 1 Corinthians 12, Ephesians 3:6, Ephesians 4). What Paul does specifically discuss here are relationships so intimate and so interconnected that they are like a body; even a body doing just what I described my right leg doing for my left ankle. Let's take a look at Galatians 6:1-10, focusing on the relationship to which God is calling his readers and children.

Read Galatians 6:1-3

1.	What are we to do when we see someone caught in sin?

2.	How are we to do it?

3.	What are we to do with ourselves as we engage in the above?

4.	In Galatians 6:2, what do you think he means saying that our above actions fulfill the law of Christ?

5.	Sum up in one word what can fulfill the law of Christ.

It is so cool that we find ourselves back to the idea of love again. Even though the word is not actually mentioned here, the actions that God tells us to take toward the struggling are all about love! I'm always encouraged to read consistent and repeated themes all the way through God's word. The love in these verses is not unlike the actions of love that we looked at from 1 Corinthians and Romans in previous days' study. It's not the easy kind of, "I feel so good about you," love. It is the "doing hard things for the good of another person" love.

As I think about the actions of love here; specifically helping someone "caught" up, a pretty disgusting image comes to mind. In fact, I'm sorry to take us here at this point, especially for those arachnophobes among us, but here we go. If you need to, just keep thinking about love, love, love as we delve into what these difficult actions of love look like here. As I read these verses about someone being caught in sin, and the gentle way with which we get involved and help, I'm sorry to say, I think of removing someone tangled in spider web.

If you are already experiencing tingly head or crawling skin, skip this next paragraph. You get the idea anyway. If you're still with me, have you ever seen or touched the web of a Black Widow? It is so strong and so sticky that you could identify the Black Widow as the web's maker, without even seeing the spider. That is what Paul's words remind me of here. Sin is sticky. It's easy to get tangled, trapped, and completely and helplessly stuck. It takes great care, gentleness and time to help someone out. Not only that, but I think of what it's like to touch that sticky web. The spider might notice and come close. The web gets on your fingers. You could end up bitten or walk away with gossamers dangling! That just ain't pretty! This is difficult and delicate work and it's no joke. Paul reminds us not to get too comfortable or we might just end up in the web too!

If I lost you at spider, welcome back! The point is: loving someone caught in sin can be sticky and dangerous. We must be careful. We must stay connected to the whole body. Don't go it alone or you too can get caught. The body, under the control of the head, Jesus, will work to keep each part together. Solo, we don't stand a chance!

Let's take a look at what each part of the body functioning and doing its part looks like. Read Galatians 6:3-5

6.   What does Paul say could be the result if we try to help someone caught in sin while relying on our own abilities and goodness?

7.   What is the truth we find in verse 3 when someone depends too highly on themselves and their own abilities?

8.   From verse 4, how can we keep a realistic perspective of who we are?

9.   What do these verses say about comparing ourselves to others?

This is serious business. It's family business. It's body business. We are to be like my right leg to my left ankle. We are to help bear the burden of one that is not healthy. After a while, though, my compensating knee felt the weight and pain of carrying the burden. It could not be the ankle; it could only help. If it tried to take over for the ankle long term, it was bound to be injured too. The right knee isn't all that! It's a great right knee and sure, carried the burden when the ankle needed help, but it couldn't depend on itself to be both. At some point, the ankle improved from the rest given by the knee and then both the ankle and the knee went back to doing what they do best. The ankle being an ankle and the knee being a knee! I broke my toe a few weeks ago and we are not even going there!

This passage can also seem a little confusing as it seems like Paul is telling them to carry someone's burden in one verse and then a few verses later to only carry their own load. I recently heard a lovely explanation for this in a sermon on this passage from our church's Lead Pastor, Carl Sutter. Pastor Sutter explained that the burden in verse 2 could be defined as something that was "oppressive" or more than a person could bear. This term defined someone in trouble and over their head. Hence they are "caught" in sin. They can't find, dig, cut, scratch or claw their way out. They need help, gentle as it may be. Pastor Sutter further explained that the term "load" in verse five, was that which we are all capable of carrying. It is like a responsibility. It is what we are made for and competent to do. Just like my ankle and knee. The knee helped when the ankle was incapable, but when the time came, the knee and the ankle went back to doing what they were made for.

Verses 6-10 continue to explain our role in love as a body. Read Galatians 6:6

10. What does Paul say the Galatians should share with those who teach?

The NIV Study Notes indicate that Paul meant that they should share financially with those who teach.

11. Based on Galatians 6:8-9 what are the consequences of our actions?

12. According to verse 10, to whom are we to take special opportunities to do good?

13.   List actions you think could fall into the category of "doing good."

We can see from the whole of the passage that we have studied today that we are intimately connected and what we do has consequences. These consequences not only affect us, but the entire body, as we are one working together. Thankfully, we have a good head on our shoulders! We know that head of our body is quite literally Jesus Christ! Knowing that gives us hope of having a functional body, even a good one, a beautiful one and a strong one. Sometimes, parts of the body are going to be down. He's given us instruction on how to help get that part up and running again without breaking the other parts down in the process. That's good, good, isn't it! Our true body has hope. I can't say the same for my poor little injured toe!

The Point:

We are all in this together working toward the goal of eternal life. We can't work for it on our own, but rather through Jesus. In fact, He is the head of the body, of which we are all parts. We work together, help each other, let him keep our selves healthy and then we will be supported as we work to live for his Spirit.

The Questions:

1. When you see another person "caught in a sin" what is your usual response? Do you try to restore them, help them gently, judge, condemn? How do your actions support your answer?

2. What are some specific ways to help gently restore another person?

3. Are there areas that you know you need to "watch out for" when helping another person who is caught? What are these? Are you connected to the body in these areas?

4. If you're part of a body and you aren't carrying your own load, what could happen?

5. What do you share ("all good things") with those who lead and instruct you in the Word?

6. Summarize Galatians 6:7-10. Why do you think Paul says "Do not be deceived: God cannot be mocked?"

7. List some ways you can "do good" to the family of believers.

LETTERS TO YOUR CHILDREN

Read Galatians 6:11-18

Wow! Here we are. We have come to the close of Paul's letter to the Galatians. And what a passionate and personal conclusion. We've already seen Paul take a parental and intimate tone. Here is no different. As I read these closing words, I cannot help but think about communication with my children or loved ones.

I consider a handwritten note, card or letter to be a treasure. My personal handwriting is actually quite unattractive. I always envied women with pretty handwriting. Nonetheless, I could not stomach the idea of typing an intimate letter to my children or husband. If I have something intimate to express to my family in writing, there's no way I would type it. I'd write it. Why? Because, unattractive or not, my handwriting is unique to me. It comes from me and is uniquely mine and therefore, it is more intimate and personal. I can relate to what Paul writes here to the Galatians. I'm sure you can too.

In these verses, Paul lets his family know that he has something intimate and important to say. He wants them to take special note of the words to come. He writes it!

Let's look at these intimate closing words.

Read Galatians 6:11. Here we read that Paul is writing these words himself. The fact that he points this out to his readers reveals that he wants them to take note of this. He is not using a secretary or scribe here.

It's interesting to note that some commentators believe that Galatians 6:11 refers to that specific verse and the text that follows, but does not include the previous chapters and verses. Some have speculated that Paul mentions the large letters because he has difficulty with his eyesight and others speculate that Paul calls out his use of large letters in order to direct the readers' attention to what follows.

1.   Why do you think Paul makes a point of telling his readers that he is writing this himself?

As we continue on, reading verses 12-16, the seriousness of what Paul is communicating is evident, but it also makes me chuckle (internally) just a little bit. We will look at what Paul is saying specifically in just a moment, but before we do, take some time to read Galatians 6:11-18.

Why is this chuckle worthy? Well, because I have a teenager! He knows that when I want him to hear something, and really "get" it, I'm going to say the same thing 15 different ways! In fact, we have a running joke, borrowed from another teenager, about the fact that I should just number my lectures. Since I'm going to repeat a theme or "lecture" over and over, I might as well save time and

assign it a number! For example: "your self-worth is based on what Jesus thinks you are worth, which is his very life," is #1. "Soda is bad for you," is number 4.

In the case of Galatians, I don't think lecture is necessarily the right word for how Paul is communicating God's words, but I do notice a theme that is repeated from his letter. He's already told them he's writing this himself, in his own handwriting, so he wants them to get it.

2.   What theme do you find here that is repeated from previous chapters?

We've read this idea over and over again. I think we could call this Galatians lecture #1. It's not what we do or what we look like. It's what Jesus did and is doing and that we are in him. It's not about being religious; it's about loving in faith. #1 is pretty good! I think I'll try it out on my boy.

Let's dig into these words a little more. God has had Paul repeat this theme throughout the letter, so we know it must be something he wants them and us to get!

We are going to spend a little time looking at the Judaizers and more specifically, the contrast between the Judaizers, who were false teachers, living a lie, and Paul, who was teaching and living the truth.

3.   List 2 negative things you learn about the Judaizers from verse 11.

4. Based on verse 13, how successful are those who are circumcised at in doing right all the time?

5. What is their goal in having the Galatians chose this outward symbol of following the law?

6. Based on Galatians 6:12-16 write the contrast between Paul and the Judaizers in the following areas:

	Judaizers	Paul
Persecution:		
Boasting:		
Righteousness:		
Body:		
Relationship with Galatians:		

Paul sums these people up pretty succinctly here! We learn that they really just want to look good on the outside and that they want to avoid persecution. In all honesty, who couldn't relate to both of those wants? I want to look good and really don't want to be persecuted! We know however, that if Jesus was persecuted, which he was, then his followers can expect it. (See Philippians 1:29-30 for more. Here we learn that both belief and suffering for

Jesus are "granted" to us.) We also know that although people look at the outward appearance, God looks at the heart. (1 Samuel 16:7) These ideas of suffering/persecution for Jesus and being concerned about how we truly are internally, are hard ideas. They aren't human nature. What Paul says then in verse 14-15 stands out in becoming the opposite of what is natural to us as humans.

7.　　What does Paul say is his relationship to the world?

8.　　What does Paul boast about?

There we have it. "Lecture" number one from Paul to the Galatians. It's all and always about Jesus! He did and does the work of crucifixion so that we could be a new creation. He makes us clean and powerful on the inside so that we will produce and grow fruit of love on the outside. It's not about our religion, it's about his love!

The Point:

Although the Judaizers were trying hard to convince the Galatians to submit to the law, they themselves were not clean on the inside. They cared about how they looked on the outside and about avoiding being persecuted. What they looked like was not at all what really mattered. What really mattered was a relationship with Jesus, who cleanses a person on the inside by his grace.

The Questions:

1. Are you, like Paul, personally invested with people with whom you share the good news about Jesus? How do your actions show this?

2. Do you know religious people who in the end only care about what they look like? How influential have they been in the kingdom of God?

3. Where do you care about looking good; on the inside or outside? How does the way you spend your time and resources support your answer?

4. What do you boast or brag about? Kids? Intellect? Talents? Good stuff you do? Jesus? How does the way you use your words support your answer?

5. Why do you think Paul closed the letter with the salutation of grace?

Let's do the same. Grace. Grace. Grace in Jesus!

SUM IT UP

Read Galatians 1:1-6:18

God's word is so deep isn't it! We could go back through just this one letter and read it countless times and it would never get stale nor stagnant! Just to recall some of the things that God brought to your mind throughout this study, go back through the previous chapters and write down either a main idea or point from each.

    1.   Galatians Chapter 1:

    2.   Galatians Chapter 2:

3.   Galatians Chapter 3:

4.   Galatians Chapter 4:

5.   Galatians Chapter 5:

6.   Galatians Chapter 6:

As I review God's words, I'm reminded and convicted. I'm reminded that my identity is in Jesus! It doesn't matter if I look religious. It matters if I look like him. I'm reminded that I have hope because he truly knows me and loves me. I'm reminded that I'm part of a promise made by him which depends on his goodness, not mine. I'm convicted to take action, in love, and more specifically, in his love. That's what counts! I'm convicted to act and pray on what he has taught me, and just as God through Paul encouraged and blessed the Galatians, I'm encouraged to go forth in grace!

7.   What will you act and pray on from God's words in Galatians?

Galatians 6:18
The grace of our Lord Jesus Christ be with your spirit, brothers. Amen. (ESV)

www.ingramcontent.com/pod-product-compliance
Lightning Source LLC
Chambersburg PA
CBHW081226040426
42445CB00016B/1903